Every Kid's Guide to
Handling
Family Arguments

Written by
JOY BERRY

CHILDRENS PRESS ®
CHICAGO

About the Author and Publisher

Joy Berry's mission in life is to help families cope with everyday problems and to help children become competent, responsible, happy individuals. To achieve her goal, she has written over two hundred self-help books for children from birth through age twelve. Her work revolutionized children's publishing by providing families with practical, how-to, living skills information that was previously unavailable in children's books.

Joy gathered a dedicated team of experts, including psychologists, educators, child developmentalists, writers, editors, designers, and artists, to form her publishing company and to help produce her work.

The company, Living Skills Press, produces thoroughly researched books and audio-visual materials that successfully combine humor and education to teach subjects ranging from how to clean a bedroom to how to resolve problems and get along with other people.

Managing Editor: Ellen Klarberg
Copy Editor: Kate Dickey
Contributing Editors: Libby Byers, Nancy Cochran, Maureen Dryden, Yona Flemming, Kathleen Mohr, Susan Motycka
Editorial Assistant: Sandy Passarino

Art Director: Laurie Westdahl
Design: Abigail Johnston, Laurie Westdahl
Production: Abigail Johnston, Caroline Rennard
Illustrations designed by: Bartholomew
Inker: Berenice Happe Iriks
Colorer: Berenice Happe Iriks
Composition: Curt Chelin

A family argument can be a positive or negative experience.

EVERY KID'S GUIDE TO HANDLING FAMILY ARGUMENTS can help you make family arguments a positive experience by teaching you the following:

- what an argument is,
- what causes arguments,
- what makes family arguments helpful, and
- what keeps family arguments to a minimum.

A family is two or more people who are related to each other. Family members usually live together in the same place.

They often eat, sleep, work, or play together.
They laugh and cry together.
They also argue with each other.

Arguments are disagreements. Sometimes they can be *angry* disagreements. Arguments are a normal part of family life.

Brothers and sisters argue with each other.
Parents argue with each other.
Parents and children argue with each other.

There are several things that upset brothers and sisters and cause them to argue.

Jealousy causes brothers and sisters to argue.

Competition also causes brothers and sisters to argue.

Teasing causes brothers and sisters to argue.

Hurting each other's bodies or feelings also causes brothers and sisters to argue.

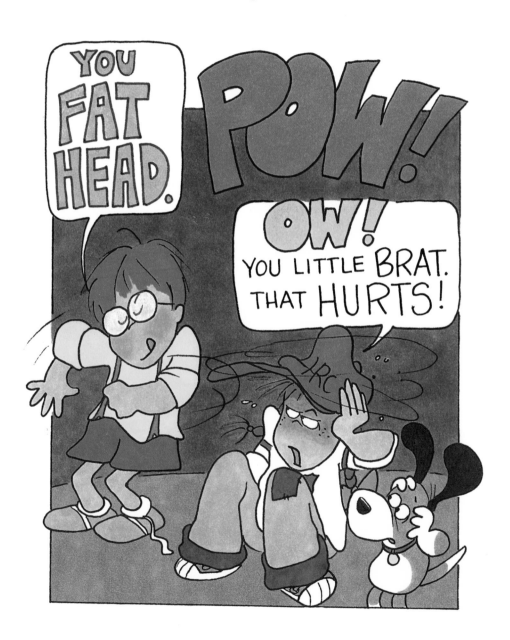

Parents argue with each other about many different subjects. Sometimes parents argue about *how their children should be raised.*

Parents sometimes argue about *how the family's money should be used.*

Sometimes parents argue about *what tasks each parent should do.*

Parents sometimes argue about *what activities the family should or should not do*.

Parents and children argue with each other about many different subjects.

Sometimes parents and children fight over *whom the children should and should not spend time with*.

Parents and children sometimes argue over *what the children should and should not do.*

Sometimes parents and children argue about *what the children can and cannot have.*

Parents and children sometimes argue about *when and where the children should go.*

Being together too much might cause family members
to argue with each other. Sometimes family members
spend so much time together they get tired of each
other. When they get tired of each other, they might
become irritated and show their irritation by
arguing.

It is safer to fight with a member of your family than with a friend. Friends can stop being friends, but family members cannot stop being family members. Mothers, fathers, brothers, and sisters will always be mothers, fathers, brothers, and sisters no matter what happens. Thus, when people are angry or upset, they often argue with family members. They feel there is no danger of losing them.

No matter what causes family arguments, they are either harmful or helpful.

Family arguments are harmful if
- someone is hurt physically,
- someone's feelings are badly hurt, or
- something is damaged or destroyed.

Family arguments are helpful if
- family members are allowed to say what is upsetting them,
- problems are dealt with and resolved, or
- family members learn valuable lessons.

Family arguments are helpful rather than harmful if family members remember:

It is OK to argue.

People who argue are not strange or bad.

When people argue, it does not mean they do not love each other.

When two people argue, it does not always mean one person is right and the other person is wrong.

You can help make the family arguments in which you are involved helpful rather than harmful by following these four steps:

Step 1. Think about the situation.

Get it clear in your mind exactly what is bothering you. You might want to do this alone or . . .

. . .you might want to ask another person to help you. Talk to someone other than the person with whom you are fighting. Another person might be able to help you figure out what is causing the argument and what can be done to resolve it.

Step 2. Listen to the person with whom you are arguing.

Try to learn exactly what he or she feels about the situation. Try to understand why the person thinks the way he or she does. It will help if you put yourself in the other person's place.

When you listen, it is important that you
- face the person,
- look directly into the person's eyes, and
- concentrate on what the person is saying.

It is also important that you do *not*
- interrupt or
- decide whether the person is right or wrong before
  he or she finishes talking.

Step 3. Share your thoughts and feelings with the person with whom you are arguing.

Tell the person exactly what is bothering you. It is important that you share your thoughts and feelings honestly. Try not to
- say things that are not true or
- hide the way you feel.

It is also important that you share your thoughts and feelings in a kind way. Try not to

- scream or yell,
- act as if you are going to hurt the person physically,
- act as if you are going to damage the person's belongings, or
- say things for the purpose of hurting the other person's feelings.

It will help if you talk about *your* thoughts and feelings rather than the thoughts and behavior of the other person.

Step 4. Do whatever you can to resolve the argument.

There are at least four ways to resolve family arguments that involve you.

The other person does what you want him or her to do.

This works only if the other person does what you want because

- the person honestly thinks it is the right thing to do and
- the person wants to cooperate with you.

People do not do their best unless

- they think they are doing the right thing and
- they are doing what they choose to do.

Getting your way is not enjoyable for you if the other person does not feel good about doing what you want. Other people can resent you for forcing them to cooperate. Their feelings of resentment can cause you to feel uncomfortable.

You must remember that getting your way is not the only way to resolve a family argument.

You do what the person wants you to do.
To make this work, you must do what the other person wants because

- you think it is the right thing to do and
- you want to cooperate with the person.

When you feel this way, you will do your best and will not be resentful.

You compromise with the other person.

When you compromise, you give in a little without giving in completely. To make this work

- you must do something the other person wants you to do and
- the other person must do something you want him or her to do.

Whatever is done must be done willingly if the compromise is to work.

You and the other person agree to disagree.
When you agree to disagree, you accept the fact that you and the other person do not feel the same way about something. To make this solution work, it is important that you

- accept that the other person has a right to think the way he or she chooses to think,
- respect the opinion of the other person,
- try not to focus on the disagreement, and
- try to focus on the things on which you do agree.

People who are involved in an argument should
resolve it themselves. This is not always possible. If
you have a difficult time resolving an argument, you
should ask someone to help you. Be sure you choose
a person who is old enough and wise enough to
- understand both sides of the argument and
- give advice that is fair to everyone involved in the
  argument.

Some family arguments do not involve you. Perhaps your parents argue with each other, or your brothers or sisters argue with each other. *Stay out of these arguments.*

To stay out of arguments that do not involve you,
you should
- avoid deciding who is right and who is wrong and
- avoid taking sides.

It will help if you do not talk about the argument
with the people who are arguing. Instead, encourage
them to talk to each other.

If you are like most people, you might experience all kinds of uncomfortable feelings when you are involved in a family argument.

You might also feel uncomfortable when other members of your family argue with each other.

Family arguments can cause you to feel uncomfortable. You should avoid starting one by following these six guidelines:

Guideline 1. Find out what the family rules are, and follow them.

Guideline 2. Respect other people's rights.

Remember that all members of your family have the
right to
- be their own person,
- be honest,
- have their basic needs met,
- ask questions and receive honest answers,
- think their own thoughts and believe their own
  beliefs,
- make mistakes,
- contribute to any decisions that affect them,
- own their own belongings,
- have privacy,
- live free from fear,
- grow and develop at their own pace, and
- defend their rights if they are being taken away.

Guideline 3. Do not talk to a family member about a sensitive subject when you are tired or in a bad mood.

Guideline 4. Do not talk to family members about sensitive subjects when they are tired or in a bad mood.

Guideline 5. Remember that no one, including you, is perfect.

No one can be right all of the time.

Guideline 6. Admit you are wrong when you are wrong.

You also need to say you are sorry and really mean it.

Often family arguments can be avoided, but sometimes they cannot.

When family arguments occur, they should be handled properly so they have a positive rather than a negative effect on everyone in the family.